GUARDIANS
OF THE
BOTTOM LINE

GUARDIANS
OF THE
BOTTOM LINE

DEMYSTIFYING CYBERSECURITY
FOR TODAY'S LEADERS

BRENDA TAYLOR, MS, PMP
JONATHAN COX, BS, CISSP, CASP

ARCHWAY
PUBLISHING

Archway Publishing books may be ordered through booksellers or by contacting:

Archway Publishing
1663 Liberty Drive
Bloomington, IN 47403
www.archwaypublishing.com
844-669-3957

ISBN: 978-1-6657-7515-1 (sc)
ISBN: 978-1-6657-7516-8 (e)

Library of Congress Control Number: 2025905534

Print information available on the last page.

Archway Publishing rev. date: 03/21/2025

CONTENTS

INTRODUCTION

In today's digital world, cyber security is not an option but a necessity for any business that wants to survive and thrive. Cyber security is the practice of protecting information systems, networks, devices, and data from unauthorized access, use, or damage. It is not just a technical issue but also a business issue, as it affects a company's reputation, profitability, and continuity.

If you are reading this, you or your company are considering rounding out your cyber security practices. This book is meant for leaders at or below the C Suite, executives, and senior managers with limited Cyber Security experience. It is being written to help you understand why Cyber Security is important, and what is required to implement an effective plan. If you are a Security Professional, this book can help you develop your overall Cyber Security plan. A Cyber Security Plan is a document that outlines the goals, strategies, policies, and procedures for cyber security in a company. It helps a company identify its overall risk profile, manage it, and respond to and recover from cyber risks/incidents and attacks. A Cyber Security Plan can help a company comply with relevant laws and regulations and communicate with stakeholders about cybersecurity issues.

AWARENESS

🔓 WHY IS HAVING A ROBUST CYBER SECURITY PLAN VITAL TO YOUR COMPANY'S SUCCESS?

Every day, companies are bombarded with increased threats, cybercriminals are constantly searching for ways to steal sensitive or personal information they can ransom or sell. Sometimes, it seems almost impossible to keep up, but that is precisely what you need to do. Your company's information, reputation, and data depend on it. The following information will explain why having a robust Cyber Security Plan is vital to your company and why it should be a pivotal part of your organization's Risk Management Plan.

Protection of Sensitive Information: Your company may have sensitive or personal information, including customer data, financial information, and intellectual property. This information is valuable to cybercriminals, who may try to steal and sell it, ransom it back to you, or destroy it to benefit your competitors. A Cyber Security Plan can help you protect your information from these threats and mitigate any residual risk of unauthorized access, use, or disclosure of your information.

Maintaining Customer Trust: Security incidents or data breaches can erode customer trust and loyalty. Customers expect you to protect their data and privacy, and to provide them with secure and reliable services. Creating a robust Cyber Security Plan demonstrates your commitment to cyber security and your respect for your customers. It also helps you to maintain a positive reputation and a competitive edge in the market.

Regulatory Compliance: Depending on your industry, location, and customer base, you may be subject to various compliance standards and regulations regarding data protection and cyber security. For example, you may need to comply with the General Data Protection Regulation (GDPR) in the European Union[1], the Health Insurance Portability and Accountability Act (HIPAA) in the United States[2], or the Personal Information Protection and Electronic Documents Act (PIPEDA) in Canada[3]. A Cyber Security Plan can help you to comply with these regulations and to avoid legal consequences or fines.

Preventing Financial Loss: Cyberattacks can cause economic loss to your company in many ways, such as theft, fraud, extortion, or litigation. Cyberattacks can also disrupt your business operations, leading to downtime, lost productivity, and lost revenue. A Cyber Security Plan can help you prevent or reduce the monetary impact by implementing detection and prevention tools and risk transference practices.

Business Continuity: Cyberattacks can disrupt your business operations, leading to downtime, lost productivity, and lost revenue. They can also damage your infrastructure, equipment, or data, making it difficult or impossible to resume normal operations. A Cyber Security Plan can help you ensure business continuity by implementing recovery and restoration measures, such as backups, disaster recovery plans, and incident response plans.

Preserving Operational Integrity: A Cyber Security Plan is an essential way for a company to help maintain and preserve the integrity of its systems, networks, and infrastructure assets, preventing disruptions and ensuring service reliability.

Protection Against Insider Threats: Cyber threats do not always come from the outside, sometimes they can come from inside your company, whether intentional or unintentional. Insider threats can include employees, contractors, partners, or vendors who have access to your information systems, networks, devices, or data. Insider threats can cause damage to your company by leaking, stealing, sabotaging, or misusing your information or resources. A Cyber Security Plan can help you to protect against insider threats by implementing security policies, procedures, and training, as well as monitoring and auditing activities.

Managing Supply Chain Risks: Beyond your organization is the entire supply chain. Your company needs to ensure that your suppliers, vendors, and partners also adhere to their own Cyber Security Plan to prevent supply chain threats. Threats that could expose your companies' data through their systems.

Having robust Cyber Security is essential to your company's Risk Management Plan. It is not only a technical issue but also a business issue, as it can help you protect sensitive information, maintain customer trust, comply with regulations, manage your company's reputation, ensure business continuity, and much more. Creating and implementing a Cyber Security Plan for your company is not a one-time event but an ongoing process that requires commitment, collaboration, and continuous improvement. By following the steps outlined in this book, we can help you create a plan for your company that moves you towards achieving your cyber security goals and objectives.

🔓 TYPES OF CYBERATTACKS

There are several types of cyberattacks, and each attack is designed to exploit vulnerabilities or achieve a particular objective. These are only a few, there are more every day, but we wanted to start to get you familiar with some of the terms used when discussing Cyber Security.

Phishing – This involves tricking people into disclosing information such as financial details, usernames, or passwords. This is normally done through deceptive emails, websites or text messages that are created to appear normal.

Ransomware – These attacks involve encrypting a victim's data and then demanding a ransom for the decryption key. This could result in data loss and operational disruption.

Malware – This includes several types of malicious software such as viruses, worms, trojans, spyware, adware, rootkits, and keyloggers. This is a term to use interchangeably with any of the previous types as a more generalized term it defines any malicious software used against any information system.

Social Engineering – This type of attack tries to manipulate individuals into providing confidential information or performing actions that may compromise security.

Whaling – This is a more sophisticated form of phishing, where the cyber attackers are targeting individuals or "big fish" within an organization such as C Suite executives or higher-ranking personnel with elevated privileges.

The next set of Cyber Attack types are not as well-known as the ones previously listed but warrant the space here, to at least be listed and defined so that you are aware that they are there and can potentially impact your company.

Man-in-the-Middle (MitM) Attacks – This type of attack is where an attacker intercepts or even alters communication between parties without their knowledge. Attackers use this to manipulate communications or eavesdrop on sensitive or confidential information.

Denial-of-Service (DoS) Attacks – This type of attack is an attempt to overwhelm networks, or systems with traffic, causing these systems to become unavailable or extremely slow.

SQL Injection – This attack tries to inject malicious SQL code into databases, exploiting vulnerabilities in web applications that use SQL queries to function.

Zero-Day Exploits – This attack targets vulnerabilities in hardware or software that are not yet known by the vendor and has not yet been patched.

Credential Stuffing – Attackers use stolen username and password combinations to gain unauthorized access to other accounts by exploiting users who reuse credentials across multiple platforms.

Typo squatting – These attacks rely on registering domain names similar to legitimate ones with the expectation that users will mistype

URLs. Once they visit the wrong site, they may be exposed to malware or phishing.

IoT Exploitation – With the growth and expansion of Internet of Things (IoT) devices, attackers may exploit vulnerabilities in connected devices to gain unauthorized access.

It's important to understand that these threats will continue to evolve and become more sophisticated, especially with the advent of AI. Cybercriminals have the advantage over businesses and individuals. Cybercriminals only need to find that one vulnerability, yet we must constantly work to protect ourselves and our data from an ever-changing landscape.

🔓 NOTABLE CASES OF CYBER SECURITY BREACHES

Here are a few important examples of cyber security attacks that have affected large companies with significant impacts on their customers, some examples of these impacts are loss of sensitive information, damaging customer trust, and financial loss. The reason that these are being listed is so the reader can understand how large and impactful a cyber breach can be, and how important it is to take the appropriate steps to protect your assets.

First American Financial Corp: In May 2019, First American Financial Corp. suffered a data leak due to poor data security and unsecure website design. Approximately 885 million files were exposed, including sensitive information such as bank account numbers, statements, mortgage payments, wire transfers, and driver's licenses. The company was fined $500,000 for this breach[4].

Microsoft: In January 2021, Microsoft disclosed a massive cyberattack on its Exchange email servers, which affected tens of thousands of organizations worldwide. The attackers exploited four vulnerabilities that allowed them to access emails and install malware on the servers. The victims included local governments, small businesses, schools, hospitals, and other entities that rely on Microsoft's email service. The attack was attributed to a Chinese state-sponsored hacking group called Hafnium, which has a history of targeting US-based organizations. Microsoft released patches to fix the vulnerabilities, but many organizations were already compromised and had to deal with the aftermath of the breach[5].

Facebook: In April 2021, Facebook suffered a data breach that exposed the sensitive personal data, account information, and passwords of 530 million users. Additionally, information was leaked to the public that in March of 2019, Facebook employees had access to 600 million user accounts and passwords. Facebook claimed that no information was exposed. This incident had a significant impact on the protection of sensitive information and maintaining customer trust[6].

Colonial Pipeline (2021): In May 2021, Colonial Pipeline, which operates critical infrastructure for the U.S. fuel supply, suffered a ransomware attack that disrupted its operations. This led to a temporary shutdown of the pipeline and impacted fuel distribution in the southeastern United States. This incident had a significant impact on maintaining customer trust, preventing monetary loss, ensuring business continuity, managing supply chain risk, and preserving operational integrity[7].

Real Estate Wealth Network (2023): In December 2023, a security researcher discovered an unsecured database belonging to Real Estate Wealth Network, a company that provides online courses and software for real estate investors. The database contained a terabyte of data, exposing sensitive personal data, property history, mortgage information, buyer and seller information, tax IDs, and other tax information. The data belonged to millions of customers and potential customers of the company, as well as thousands of real estate agents and brokers. The database and system files were not password-protected, making them accessible to anyone on the internet. The researcher notified the company but did not receive a response. The database was eventually taken offline, but the extent of the data leak and its potential consequences are unknown[8].

Change Healthcare Cyberattack (2024): In February 2024, there was a significant healthcare cyberattack that targeted Change Healthcare, a major health technology company that handles a substantial portion of the U.S. healthcare system's claims processing and payments. This incident, which began on February 21, 2024, was one of the most severe cyberattacks on the U.S. healthcare system, disrupting services and impacting hospitals, pharmacies, and other healthcare providers nationwide. The attack paralyzed health care payments, preventing hospitals and healthcare providers from submitting claims and receiving payments, which caused cash flow issues and operational disruptions. The American Hospital Association called it the most significant cyberattack against the country's healthcare system in history. Although the effect of this breach is still being analyzed, in a press release from United Health Group they indicated the overall potential extent of this breach "Based on initial targeted data sampling to date, the company has found files containing protected health information (PHI) or personally identifiable information (PII), which could cover a substantial proportion of people in America."[9]

Cyber security threats are constantly evolving and becoming more sophisticated, posing significant challenges for individuals, businesses, and governments. No one is immune to cyber security threats, and even the most sophisticated software can be impacted by an insider threat or a third-party vendor that doesn't have a robust Cyber Security Plan in place. It is a complicated problem that warrants attention. This section has shown you just a few examples of large companies that were impacted by cyberattacks and how their customers were impacted, but keep in mind, these attacks are happening every day, these are not isolated incidents.

🔓 THE HUMAN FACTOR IN CYBER SECURITY

Cybersecurity attacks are not only a threat to technology, but also to people. Employees, business leaders, customers, suppliers, and vendors can be affected by a cyberattack in many ways, such as compromised personal information, loss of confidence, increased stress, job insecurity, social engineering, and phishing threats. These impacts can have profound consequences for the well-being, productivity, and reputation of a company and its employees. It is important to understand human factors, to effectively prevent and mitigate the effects of a cyberattack on people.

Compromised Personal Information: Exposure of sensitive personal information of employees, such as names, addresses, social security numbers, bank accounts, or health records can lead to economic loss, identity theft, fraud, or blackmail. Employees may also face legal or regulatory issues if their personal information is used for illegal purposes.

Loss of Confidence: Damage to the trust and confidence that employees, business leaders, customers, suppliers, and vendors have in a company's ability to protect their data and privacy, can result in low morale, dissatisfaction, turnover, or loss of business. Harm to a company's reputation and brand image, caused by a loss of confidence, can make it harder to attract and retain talent, customers, and partners.

Increased Stress: The additional work and pressure for IT and support staff, who respond to the incidents, restore systems, and communicate with affected parties, can cause stress, burnout, fatigue, or even errors. Depending on the type of cyberattack, you could see an increase anxiety and fear among employees, who may worry about the security of their data, the stability of their jobs, or the consequences of the attack.

Job Insecurity: The financial implications could be significant for a company affected by a cyberattack, include things like loss of revenue, fines, lawsuits, or compensation claims. The fiscal impact could affect a company's budget, profitability, and growth, forcing them to implement cost-cutting measures, such as layoffs, salary reductions, or hiring freezes. This can create uncertainty and insecurity among employees, who may fear losing their jobs or income.

Social Engineering and Phishing Threats: Exploitation of the human vulnerabilities of employees, such as curiosity, greed, or empathy through the use social engineering techniques increase the possibility of a cyber incident. Criminals use tools such as impersonation, deception, or manipulation, to trick employees into revealing sensitive information, clicking on malicious links, or downloading malware. Insider threats make up a large majority of the overall cybersecurity threat risk.

Training and Cybersecurity Awareness Gaps: Training and awareness gaps among employees, who may not know how to recognize, prevent, or report a cyberattack allows a cybercriminal to exploit the gaps in the company's cybersecurity policies, procedures, or culture, which may not provide clear guidance, expectations, or incentives for employees to follow best practices.

Employee Accountability: A lack of clear policies and procedures for employee accountability in the overall Cyber Security Plan can lead to security lapses and a lack of adherence to protocols. This book recommends establishing and maintaining a strong cybersecurity posture, transparent communication, and honesty. By being proactive with employees, business leaders, customers, suppliers, and vendors about your company's cybersecurity policies and procedures you foster a culture of trust and collaboration.

A poor Cyber Security Plan or the lack of one can impact your employees. Employees rely on leadership to make the right calls and to do the right thing; in this case, which means ensuring your company's information is protected. Once an employee is hired and gives you their information, this is done with the implicit understanding that their data is held private and protected. The same applies to any information managed or maintained by your internal systems for customers, suppliers, or vendors. It is the job of a true leader to make sure that employee trust and data integrity is a top priority.

🔓 FRAMEWORKS

A Framework is a set of guidelines and practices designed to help organizations improve their cybersecurity posture. It consists of three primary components:

Core: This is a set of cybersecurity activities, outcomes, and informative references that are common across critical infrastructure sectors. The Core presents five concurrent and continuous functions—Identify, Protect, Detect, Respond, and Recover—that provide a high-level, strategic view of the lifecycle of an organization's management of cybersecurity risk.

Implementation Tiers/ Organizational Profiles: These provide context on how an organization views cybersecurity risk and the processes in place to manage that risk. The Tiers range from Partial (Tier 1) to Adaptive (Tier 4), describing an increasing degree of rigor and sophistication in cybersecurity risk management practices.

Profiles: These are unique alignments of the Core functions, categories, and subcategories with the business requirements, risk tolerance, and resources of the organization. Profiles help organizations to align their cybersecurity activities with their business requirements, risk tolerance, and resources.

The NIST 2.0 Cybersecurity Framework, also known as the NIST CSF 2.0 is an example of a Framework used by many companies and corporations to set up the Cyber Security Plans.[10]

IDENTIFICATION

🔓 CONTEXT, CRITICALITY, AND RISK LEVELS

The initial step in the creation of a Cyber Security Plan is Identification. This step is important because the information gathered helps the company make informed decisions to manage cybersecurity risks and align cybersecurity efforts with business needs and goals. By addressing the following categories, organizations can build a comprehensive picture of their cybersecurity posture, identify where improvements are needed, and prioritize actions to reduce risk.

Governance: The organization's cybersecurity risk management strategy, expectations, and policy need to be established, communicated, and monitored. It should be designed to understand and assess specific cybersecurity needs, protect data, assets, and operations. This involves defining goals, assigning roles and responsibilities, identifying internal functions, utilizing external partners, such as vendors and regulators, and managing legal and regulatory requirements.

Business Environment Assessment: Understanding the business context is crucial. This means knowing the mission, objectives, stakeholders, and essential processes of the organization. As you begin the process of evaluating the business environment, it is important to not forget about internal and external dependencies, these will be key to project management functions and risk management. Key elements include defining risk appetite and tolerance, ensuring compliance with legal and industry standards, clarifying roles and responsibilities, and aligning cybersecurity initiatives with business priorities. By integrating cybersecurity into the overall business strategy, organizations can make informed decisions, allocate resources effectively, manage risks proactively, ensure regulatory compliance, and build stakeholder confidence.

Asset Management Assessment: Asset management involves tracking and managing an organization's physical and digital resources. This process includes cataloging hardware, software, data, communication systems, and understanding their interconnections. Key steps include creating an inventory of all assets, prioritizing them based on their importance and value to the organization, and defining clear roles and responsibilities for both internal staff and external partners to maintain asset security and availability. Depending on how your organization intends to organize assets it may be beneficial to establish classification levels to clearly identify importance, this could include separating proprietary data or systems from other less critical systems.

RISK MANAGEMENT

Risk Assessment - Risk assessment involves identifying and evaluating cyber related risks. This includes documenting vulnerabilities in assets that could be exploited, analyzing cyber threat intelligence, and identifying internal and external threats. Some of these internal and external threats may be things such as IT personnel retention, compromised utilities such as power or water, and even unplanned disasters to the area around your facility that could affect communication paths. Most companies may not have back up internet paths, so you are still reliant on the local area's internet connections. These are some examples of unrecognized risk, with that in mind it is important to assess these risks wholistically as an enterprise because it is likely that multiple departments or potentially all departments in your organization relay on IOT systems causing even small risk to be significant. To avoid that type of impact it is important to understand the realistic likelihood of cyber incidents, determining their risk levels, and prioritize your responses with a priority on mitigation, transference, avoidance, or acceptance of the remaining risks.

Risk Strategy - Developing a risk strategy means setting up policies, procedures, and practices that can be followed continuously with upper management buy in. This involves communication with stakeholders with the purpose of defining organizational risk tolerance based on mission, vision, and goals. Following stakeholder buy in and establishment of these tools, it will become a constant rotation of identifying new risks implementing the procedures and categorizing it appropriately for action to be take in some direction.

Supply Chain Risk Management: As organizations rely more on suppliers and third-party partners, they inherently accept additional risks. Effective cyber supply chain risk management includes identifying, prioritizing, and assessing cyber risks of suppliers and partners. This can be accomplished using establishing contractual requirements and monitoring compliance with cybersecurity standards. Due to the nature of most business it is a best practice to implement planning and testing of their systems to ensure they meet the requirements you set. This practice will allow you to know the terrain they are using allowing for a much smoother recovery effort in case an incident happens. This testing of outside entities that supply your critical business operations, should be added to your cyber security plan, along with standing Service level agreement to ensure positive confirmation of who is responsible for what in a recovery environment.

PROTECTION

🔒 HOW TO SAFEGUARD CRITICAL INFRASTRUCTURE AND DATA

Once you have taken the time to identify, assess, and clarify the risks that you need to manage as part of your Cyber Security Plan, you now need to think about how to mitigate those risks. Protecting an organization from a cybersecurity attack requires a proactive approach to mitigate those risks and vulnerabilities. Here are a few documented best practices that can help.

Establish an Incident Response Team: Cyber threats can result in significant financial losses, reputational damage, and disruption to operations. To address these risks, developing an Incident Response Team (IRT) is a key step in managing overall risk.

The primary objective of the IRT is to quickly identify, contain, and mitigate cyber threats, thereby minimizing their impact. This team will work proactively to prevent incidents and reactively, to manage them efficiently when they occur. The benefits of having an IRT are substantial, especially when you think about the potential benefits of how quickly they can bring your systems back online. Without a designated team of individuals with assigned roles and responsibilities, you may have personnel trying to help but causing more damage, or contrarily, you may have everyone thinking that someone else is managing things when it's true no one is. Having this team staffed out enhances your security posture, meets regulatory requirements, manages the overall communication in an emergency, and ensures you can resume operations efficiently.

Create an Incident Response Plan: Once you have identified incidents that may happen and identified who will respond, the next step is to decide how they respond. The key to a successful response plan is utilizing subject matter experts and industry-based lessons learned from earlier similar incidents. Development in this fashion will lead to a better, more complete understanding of variables that may come up during recovery efforts. Once you know how they will respond, you need to test the response plan. These tests can come in multiple forms, such as tabletop exercises, penetration tests, walk-throughs, and simulations.

Create an Incident Response Communication Plan: Developing an Incident Response Communication Plan ensures clear, coordinated, and prompt communication during a cybersecurity incident. This will also help control the message and maintain positive external communication, ensuring reputational integrity. By providing a structured framework for internal and external communications, the plan minimizes response time, reduces confusion, and reassures stakeholders that the situation is being managed effectively. Consistent and accurate messaging prevents misinformation and demonstrates a proactive approach to managing incidents, sustaining trust and confidence among employees, customers, partners, and regulators.

Effective Identity Management, Authentication and Access Control: This process involves issuing, managing, verifying, and auditing identities and credentials for authorized devices, users, and processes. Security vulnerabilities can arise without this function, such as unauthorized access or unsecure file systems. Physical and remote access to assets must be carefully managed to prevent unauthorized entry and ensure data integrity. Access permissions should adhere to principles like least privilege and separation of duties. Least privilege is the process of limiting user privileges to what is necessary for their roles. Separation of duties is the process of dividing system privileges so that you do not have system administrators auditing their own work. This separation also helps the change control board ensure nothing is placed into service before its approved. Additionally, protecting network integrity through proper segregation measures enhances overall cybersecurity resilience, mitigating risks posed by potential breaches and unauthorized access attempts. Integrating these practices into operational frameworks helps businesses maintain a secure and compliant environment amidst constantly evolving threats.

Promoting Awareness and Training Across Organizational Roles: Effective cybersecurity hinges on comprehensive awareness and training initiatives. It is important that all users from your front-line workers to your Senior Executives and third-party stakeholders such as suppliers and partners are fully trained. You need to ensure they are well-trained and informed in cybersecurity best practices. The training and awareness should address their roles and responsibilities in safeguarding sensitive information and mitigating risks. Senior Executives and cybersecurity personnel play pivotal role, requiring tailored training to grasp their unique responsibilities in maintaining organizational resilience against cyber threats. By fostering a culture of awareness and ensuring continuous education, businesses can significantly bolster their defenses against security breaches and compromised data.

Ensuring Comprehensive Data Security Practices: Organizations need to safeguard data both at rest and in transit through encryption and access controls to prevent unauthorized access and breaches. Formal management of assets, including during removal, transfers, and disposition, ensures data integrity and confidentiality are maintained throughout the lifecycle. Capacity planning helps sustain data availability, minimizing disruptions to business operations. Implementing measures to prevent data leaks and employing integrity checking mechanisms for software and firmware further fortify defenses against cyber threats. Separating development and testing environments from production environments helps mitigate risks associated with unauthorized modifications or compromises. Lastly ensuring your administrators and system engineers stay compliant with change control practices ensures no new vulnerabilities are implemented until they are properly secured.

Establishing Robust Information Protection Processes: Information protection processes involve establishing and maintaining a baseline configuration for IT and industrial control systems to mitigate vulnerabilities and ensure consistent operation. Implementing a system development life cycle helps manage systems from inception through retirement, ensuring security measures are integrated throughout. Rigorous configuration change control processes further enhance security by governing modifications to system configurations. Regular backups of information, coupled with periodic testing, ensure data availability and resilience against data loss incidents. System baselines are a snapshot in time that your organization agrees meets its operational and compliance requirements. Baselines should also ensure compliance with policies regarding the physical operating environment, this safeguards organizational assets against physical threats. Secure data destruction practices are crucial to prevent unauthorized access to sensitive information, including infrastructure configuration. Continual improvement of protection efforts and technologies, along with baseline management, strengthens overall cybersecurity posture.

Ensuring Effective Maintenance Practices: Timely maintenance and repair activities are logged and conducted using approved tools to uphold asset integrity and functionality. Remote maintenance procedures should be carefully managed, logged, and authorized to prevent unauthorized access and potential security breaches. These practices not only sustain operational efficiency but also minimize vulnerabilities that could compromise organizational data and systems.

Implementing Effective Validation Measures: The key to ensuring compliance management and best practices is through the review of logs. These audit logs should be meticulously determined, documented, implemented, and reviewed to track and monitor system activities effectively. The threshold for determining how to implement this practice is determined by what governance you are operating within such as HIPAA. You should also define policies restricting the use of removable media help prevent data breaches and unauthorized access. Though your log review you should be looking for events related to escalation of privilege, system configuration changes, or anything related to the scope of your attack surface. Robust data analysis of logs will further fortify defenses against potential vulnerabilities and cyber-attacks, by understanding normal operational traffic and events vs malicious traffic. These measures ensure comprehensive protection of organizational infrastructure and data, supporting operational continuity and resilience in today's dynamic threat landscape.

DETECTION

🔓 IDENTIFICATION OF CYBERSECURITY EVENTS

While Identification and Protection are key steps in the overall process, you need to develop the capability to identify and detect those events that are happening in your environment, so that you can effectively respond to those threats. The next set of key topics will talk to you about what you need to do to set up a process to help with your overall identification and detection of cybersecurity events.

Managing Anomalies and Events: Establishing and managing a baseline of network operations and expected data flows enables an organization to detect deviations that may indicate potential security incidents. Detected events are carefully analyzed to ascertain the targets and methods employed by attackers, facilitating informed responses and mitigation strategies. Integration of event data from multiple sources and sensors allows for comprehensive correlation and contextual understanding of security events, enhancing threat visibility and response capabilities. Evaluating the impact of events helps prioritize response efforts and minimize operational disruptions. Establishing incident alert thresholds ensures timely notification of potential threats, enabling proactive measures to mitigate risks and protect organizational assets.

Ensuring Effective Security through Continuous Monitoring: Security focused continuous monitoring involves ongoing monitoring of the network, physical environment, and personnel activities to identify potential security events. Detection mechanisms for malicious code and unauthorized mobile code help mitigate risks posed by malware and unauthorized software. Monitoring external service provider activities enables visibility into potential security events originating from third-party interactions. Continuous monitoring also includes vigilant oversight for unauthorized personnel, connections, devices, and software, safeguarding against unauthorized access and potential breaches. Regular vulnerability scans further enhance security by identifying and addressing potential weaknesses in systems and applications as they are reported industry wide. Comprehensive monitoring practices allows organizations to maintain heightened situational awareness, promptly respond to emerging threats, and bolster overall cybersecurity resilience.

Team Based Detection Processes: Clearly defining roles and responsibilities ensures accountability across various tools and activities. This teamwork enables swift and coordinated responses to potential incidents. Security teams also fill a critical role in change management to ensure compliance and detection efforts meet industry standards. Regular testing of your security team's detection capabilities verifies effectiveness and readiness to identify and mitigate emerging threats. Testing provides ensured communication of event detection information to relevant stakeholders, facilitating prompt response and mitigation strategies. Continuous improvement of detection processes helps to prepare your team to engage evolving. By prioritizing these practices, businesses can bolster their security team internally saving resources that can be used elsewhere, while still meeting requirements and meting business goals.

RESPONSE

🔓 WHAT TO DO DURING A CYBER-ATTACK

Responding quickly and effectively to a cybersecurity breach is critical to helping minimize damage, protect sensitive information, and restore normal operations. If your company has experienced a cybersecurity breach, here is an example of some of the initial steps you should take.

Activate the Incident Response Team and Execute Response Plan: As soon as a breach is detected, activate your Incident Response Team (IRT), which may consist of IT professionals, cybersecurity experts, legal advisors, and communication specialists. The team should understand roles and responsibilities for each team member, and a leader should already be determined. If the pre-determined leader or any of the other team members are not available – refer directly to the pre-defined backups. The Incident Response Plan has been developed and tested at this point and is ready for execution.

Initiate Your Incident Response Communication Plan: Clear and effective communication is pivotal during incident response to ensure coordinated and timely actions within the organization. The Incident Response Communication Plan developed earlier would have outlined what should be done in this phase. Personnel are informed of their roles and responsibilities, establishing a structured order of operations when responding to incidents. Incidents are reported promptly, facilitating swift and appropriate responses. Information sharing follows the Incident Communication Plan, ensuring relevant stakeholders are kept informed throughout the incident lifecycle. Coordination with internal and external stakeholders occurs as per the plans, fostering collaborative efforts to mitigate impacts and restore normal operations efficiently. By prioritizing communication strategies as defined in the Incident Response Communication Plan, businesses can enhance resilience, minimize disruption, and effectively manage incidents to protect organizational assets and reputation.

Engage Law Enforcement: Depending on the severity and nature of the breach, you may need to engage local law enforcement or cybercrime authorities. Consult with legal counsel before involving law enforcement and provide them with the necessary information. Cooperate with the authorities and follow their guidance.

Isolate and contain the breach! Isolate the affected systems and contain the breach to prevent further spread of the attack. Disconnect compromised devices or networks from the rest of the infrastructure to limit the attacker's access. Implement backup or alternative systems if necessary to maintain essential functions.

Preserve Evidence: Preserve digital evidence related to the breach. Document and capture relevant information, including logs, system snapshots, and any other data that may be crucial for investigating the incident and identifying the attack vector. Secure and store the evidence in a safe location.

Assess the Impact: Conduct a thorough assessment to understand the extent of the breach. Identify compromised systems, affected data, and potential vulnerabilities that were exploited. This assessment will inform the development of a remediation plan and help prevent future incidents.

Remember that every cybersecurity incident is unique, and the response may need to be tailored to the specific circumstances. It's essential to have a well-documented and regularly tested incident response plan in place to ensure a swift and effective response to a breach.

RECOVERY

🔒 HOW TO RECOVER AFTER A CYBER-ATTACK

Once you have effectively responded to the cyberattack, you need to review what happened to ensure that the same thing, or similar issues don't affect your company again. The following are a list of actions that you should review that can help you address the recovery from a cyberattack.

Implement Mitigation Measures: Take immediate steps to mitigate the impact of the breach. This may include things like applying security patches, resetting passwords, and implementing temporary workarounds to secure the environment while investigations are ongoing.

Engage External Experts: Consider engaging external cybersecurity experts or forensics professionals, if necessary. Their expertise can be valuable in identifying the root cause and implementing effective countermeasures. This step, along with the ones already outlined, can help organizations respond effectively to a cybersecurity incident.

Update Security Policies and Procedures: After a cyber-attack, it is important to review and update your security policies and procedures based on the lessons learned from the breach. This can help identify areas for improvement and implement changes to strengthen the overall cybersecurity posture of the organization. This step involves analyzing the incident response process, identifying gaps or weaknesses, and making necessary changes to prevent similar incidents from occurring in the future. This may include updating security protocols, enhancing employee training, and implementing new security measures.

Conduct a Post-Incident Analysis: After the breach is contained and normal operations are restored, it is important to conduct a comprehensive post-incident analysis. This involves identifying the root cause of the breach, evaluating the effectiveness of the response, and documenting lessons learned to enhance future incident response capabilities. The post-incident analysis can help organizations understand what went wrong, how the incident was handled, and what can be done to prevent similar incidents from occurring in the future. This information can be used to update security policies and procedures, improve employee training, and implement new security measures to strengthen the organization's overall cybersecurity posture, develop and implement long-term remediation.

SUMMARY

As you have seen, there is a critical necessity to maintain a robust cybersecurity program. This proves itself to be vital every day as threats evolve and more companies find themselves under attack. Situations like those attacks could be the last hit that brings a company to the ground, but luckily you will be prepared. Attacks WILL eventually happen but how you minimize damage and recover is what sets companies apart.

Through this book, you have seen examples of attacks that have plagued other companies, along with attack types. You have also seen best practices that will help you mitigate the risk associated with those attacks. You have even seen some ideas of how you can implement your own cyber security plan, but it is on you to put in the work to make it a success. Remember a major part cyber security is commitment to the plan and doing what you can to evolve your program, as necessary. Lastly, don't be afraid to reach out to other professionals in the IT cyber security world. It's impossible to know everything, so reach out for different perspectives when you can, these inputs can only help.

KEY TAKEAWAYS

- Cyber security is not just a technical issue, but also a business issue, as it affects the reputation, profitability, and continuity of a company.

- Creating and implementing a Cyber Security Plan for your company is not a <u>one-time event</u>, but an ongoing process that requires commitment, collaboration, and continuous improvement.

- Cybercriminals only need to find that one vulnerability, yet we must constantly work to protect ourselves and our data from an ever-changing landscape.

- Cybersecurity attacks are not only a threat to technology, but also to people.

- Employees rely on leadership to make the right calls and to do the right thing; in this case, which means ensuring your company's information is protected.

- Identification is important because the information gathered helps the company make informed decisions to manage cybersecurity risks and align cybersecurity efforts with business needs and goals in mind.

- Protecting an organization from a cybersecurity attack requires a proactive approach to mitigate those risks and vulnerabilities.

- An Incident Response Team is Key to managing and responding to risks. The primary objective of the IRT is to quickly identify, contain, and mitigate cyber threats, thereby minimizing their impact. This team will work proactively to prevent incidents and reactively, to manage them efficiently when they occur.

- Once you have effectively responded to the cyberattack, you need to review what happened to ensure that the same thing, or similar issues don't affect your company again.

APPENDIX

🔓 A – FRAMEWORKS

Cybersecurity frameworks provide guidelines and best practices, along with a structured approach to help organizations establish, implement, and maintain effective cybersecurity programs. Organizations will usually choose a cybersecurity framework based on their industry, regulatory requirements, or specific organizational needs.

Here is an example of some prominent cybersecurity frameworks as of the printing of this material:

NIST Cybersecurity Framework (CSF): Developed by the National Institute of Standards and Technology (NIST), the NIST CSF provides a voluntary framework that organizations can use to assess and improve their cybersecurity risk management. It consists of five core functions: Identify, Protect, Detect, Respond, and Recover.[11]

ISO/IEC 27001: ISO/IEC 27001 is an international standard that outlines the requirements for establishing, implementing, maintaining, and continually improving an Information Security Management System (ISMS). It covers a broad range of information security controls and best practices.[12]

CIS Critical Security Controls (CIS Controls): The Center for Internet Security (CIS) Critical Security Controls is a set of best practices designed to help organizations prioritize and implement cybersecurity measures effectively. It focuses on foundational controls to enhance cybersecurity resilience.[13]

COBIT (Control Objectives for Information and Related Technologies): COBIT is a framework developed by ISACA for the governance and management of enterprise IT. It provides a set of guidelines for aligning IT goals with business objectives, including considerations for cybersecurity and risk management.[14]

ITIL (Information Technology Infrastructure Library): ITIL is a set of practices for IT service management (ITSM) that focuses on aligning IT services with the needs of the business. While not exclusively a cybersecurity framework, it includes principles related to risk management and security incident response.[15]

CMMI Cyber Maturity Platform: The Cyber Maturity Platform, based on the Capability Maturity Model Integration (CMMI), helps organizations assess and improve their cybersecurity capabilities. It provides a maturity model to guide organizations in enhancing their cybersecurity processes.[16]

PCI DSS (Payment Card Industry Data Security Standard): PCI DSS is a set of security standards designed to ensure that all companies that accept, process, store, or transmit credit card information maintain a secure environment. It is particularly relevant to organizations handling payment card data.[17]

FAIR (Factor Analysis of Information Risk): FAIR is a framework for quantifying and managing information risk. It provides a model for understanding and analyzing cyber risk in financial terms, allowing organizations to prioritize risk mitigation efforts based on potential impact.[18]

CMMC (Cybersecurity Maturity Model Certification): Developed by the U.S. Department of Defense, CMMC is a framework designed to enhance the cybersecurity posture of defense contractors. It includes a set of maturity levels with specific cybersecurity practices and processes.[19]

ISF Standard of Good Practice for Information Security: The Information Security Forum (ISF) provides a comprehensive framework known as the Standard of Good Practice for Information Security. It covers a wide range of cybersecurity topics and provides guidance on security controls.[20]

SANS Critical Security Controls: The SANS Institute offers a set of Critical Security Controls, which provides a prioritized list of cybersecurity best practices. These controls are designed to be actionable and effective in addressing common security issues.[21]

FISMA (Federal Information Security Management Act): FISMA is a U.S. federal law that defines a framework for managing and securing federal government information and systems. It outlines requirements for agencies to develop, document, and implement information security programs.[22]

🔓 B – CERTIFICATIONS

Here are some prominent cybersecurity certifications that professionals may pursue to enhance their credentials and career opportunities (as of the printing of this material). One keynote is that most of these certifications are vendor neutral, so they don't typically emphasize any technology company. Depending on the need of your organization you can identify certifications at those companies and obtain specific certs related to your systems. However, while you are growing a team it may benefit you to look for personnel who can thrive in any environment because those individuals will be able to learn a variety of equipment or platforms faster.

CompTIA Security+ (SY0-601): A foundational certification covering essential cybersecurity concepts, Security+ is suitable for entry-level professionals. It validates knowledge in areas like network security, cryptography, and risk management.[23]

CompTIA Cybersecurity Analyst (CySA+): CySA+ is an intermediate-level certification by CompTIA that focuses on cybersecurity analytics and threat detection. It is suitable for professionals involved in cybersecurity operations and response.[24]

Certified Information Systems Security Professional (CISSP): Offered by (ISC)², the CISSP is a globally recognized certification for experienced cybersecurity professionals. It covers a broad range of security domains, including access control, cryptography, and security operations.[25]

Certified Cloud Security Professional (CCSP): Jointly offered by (ISC)² and Cloud Security Alliance (CSA), CCSP is designed for professionals with expertise in securing cloud environments. It covers cloud architecture, data security, and legal and Compliance aspects.[26]

Certified Information Security Manager (CISM): CISM offered by ISACA is designed for professionals who seek the ability to assess risks, implement effective governance, and proactively respond to incidents.[27]

Certified Information Systems Auditor (CISA): The CISA certification, offered by ISACA, is designed for professionals involved in information systems auditing and control. It emphasizes skills related to information systems audit, control, and security.[28]

Certified Incident Handler (ECIH): The EC-Council's ECIH certification focuses on incident handling and response. It covers topics such as incident handling processes, forensic analysis, and network security.[29]

Certified Ethical Hacker (CEH): EC-Council's CEH certification is designed for individuals specializing in ethical hacking and penetration testing. It covers tools and techniques used by ethical hackers to assess and secure computer systems. The Mindset of an attacker may help to identify vulnerabilities that you didn't know you had.[30]

Offensive Security Certified Professional (OSCP): Offered by Offensive Security, the OSCP certification is well-regarded in the penetration testing community. It requires candidates to complete a hands-on practical exam, demonstrating their ability to exploit and secure systems.[31]

GIAC Security Essentials Certification (GSEC): Offered by the Global Information Assurance Certification (GIAC), GSEC is a general security certification covering a wide range of topics, including network security, cryptography, and incident handling.[32]

Cisco Certified CyberOps Associate: Cisco's CyberOps Associate certification focuses on cybersecurity operations. It validates skills related to security monitoring, analysis, and incident response using Cisco technologies.[33]

Certified in Risk and Information Systems Control (CRISC): Another certification by ISACA, CRISC, is for professionals responsible for managing and mitigating IT-related business risks. It covers risk identification, assessment, response, and monitoring.[34]

AWS Certified Security - Specialty: Offered by Amazon Web Services (AWS), this certification is for professionals with expertise in securing AWS environments. It covers identity and access management, encryption, and incident response.[35]

C – SECURITY ROLES

Example of Security Roles that may benefit your organization.

CISO - Chief Information Security Office: They have a high-level security role within a company whose job is to protect a company's data and manage its IT security. They collaborate with other Senior Executives and IT security experts.

DPO - Data Protection Officer: Data protection officers (DPOs) will help monitor internal Compliance, inform, and advise on your internal data protection obligations, and provide advice regarding Data Protection Impact Assessments (DPIAs).

Security Analyst: They will monitor their organization's networks for security breaches and investigate when something occurs.

Security Engineer: They are responsible for keeping a company's security systems up and running. This involves implementing and testing new security features, planning computer and network upgrades, troubleshooting, and responding to security incidents.

Security Architect: Their job is to design, build, and maintain your company's security system.

Security Administrator: Point person for a cybersecurity team. They are usually responsible for installing, administering, and troubleshooting an organization's security solutions.

Penetration Tester: This role seeks, identifies, and attempts to breach existing weaknesses in digital systems and computing networks to help identify weaknesses.

ABOUT THE AUTHORS

Brenda Taylor, MS, PMP
President and Co-Founder of Cox Premier Consulting, LLC
https://coxpremierconsulting.com/

Brenda has over 30+ years of experience in Project, Program, and Portfolio Management. She has held a PMP certification since 2002 and received a Master's Degree in Project Management in 2004.

She has run her own Project and Program Management consulting company since 2020. Her experience is in manufacturing and healthcare industries and has extensive experience in business and large-scale IT projects. Brenda has also led numerous projects that including large-scale ERP implementations, product launches, product development, research and development projects, applications/software development, application optimization, clinical systems development, hardware/networking projects, and other various IT projects.

Jonathan Cox, BS, CISSP, CASP
Co-Founder of Cox Premier Consulting, LLC

Jonathan has over 15 years of experience in the Navy, which has given him years of experience in System administration, Network Vulnerability Assessment, and Information Security Manager roles.

He has held CISSP certification, along with CASP, Security +, Network +, Linux +, and Certified Ethical Hacker since 2018.

He has worked at multiple levels of cybersecurity administration from unit-level to enterprise-level security management and vulnerability assessment/mitigation.

Jonathan has used a variety of tools and seen many different and unique network systems which has made him familiar with configurations and best practices necessary to run a fully functional business operation.

He has also led major projects in enterprise-level system migration and upgrade, allowing them to finish on time and meet system operation expectations. These projects included dozens of tightly coupled dependent programs that require minimal resource fluctuation and high system availability.

He has also assisted in writing cybersecurity policies and best practices associated with training cybersecurity professionals at multiple levels of enterprise administration, allowing for the highest and most well-trained workforce possible.

ENDNOTES

1   EUR-Lex, "General Data Protection Regulation (GDPR)", https://eur-lex.europa.eu/legal-content/EN/TXT/?uri=CELEX%3A32016R0679, Accessed 11 June 2024.

2   U.S Department of Health and Human Service, "Health Insurance Portability and Accountability Act (HIPAA)", https://www.hhs.gov/hipaa/for-professionals/index.html, Accessed 11 June 2024.

3   Office of the Privacy Commissioner of Canada. "The Personal Information Protection and Electronic Documents Act (PIPEDA)." Office of the Privacy Commissioner of Canada, 8 December 2021, www.priv.gc.ca/en/privacy-topics/privacy-laws-in-canada/the-personal-information-protection-and-electronic-documents-act-pipeda/, Accessed 11 June 2024.

4   KrebsonSecurity, "First American Financial Corp. Leaked Hundreds of Millions of Title Insurance Records", https://krebsonsecurity.com/2019/05/first-american-financial-corp-leaked-hundreds-of-millions-of-title-insurance-records/, May 24, 2019, Accessed 11, June 2024.

    KrebsonSecurity,"SEC Investigating Data Leak at First American Financial Corp.", https://krebsonsecurity.com/2019/08/sec-investigating-data-leak-at-first-american-financial-corp/, August 12, 2019, Accessed 11, June 2024.

    KrebsonSecurity,"NY Charges First American Financial for Massive Data Leak", https://krebsonsecurity.com/2020/07/ny-charges-first-american-financial-for-massive-data-leak/. July 23, 2020, Accessed 11, June 2024.

Toulas, Bill, "First American' to Pay a Fine of Only $500,000 for the Massive 2019 Data Breach", https://www.technadu.com/first-america n-fine-only-500000-dollars-massive-2019-data-breach/284764/, June 19, 2021, Accessed 11, June 2024.

5   Wikipedia, "2021 Microsoft Exchange Server data breach", https:// en.wikipedia.org/wiki/2021 Microsoft Exchange Server data breach, Accessed 11 June 2024.

Krebs Security, "At Least 30,000 U.S. Organizations Newly Hacked Via Holes in Microsoft's Email Software", https://krebsonsecurity. com/2021/03/at-least-30000-u-s-organizations-newly- hacked-via-hole s-in-microsofts-email-software, March 5, 2021, Accessed 11 June 2024.

6   Jee, Charlotte, "What you need to know about the Facebook data leak", https://www.technologyreview.com/2021/04/07/1021892/ facebook-data-leak/, April 7, 2021, Accessed 11, June 2024.

Bowman, Emma, "After Data Breach Exposes 530 Million, Facebook Says It Will Not Notify Users", https://www.kpbs.org/news/2021/04/09/ after-data-breach-exposes-530-million-facebook/, April 9, 2021, Accessed 11, June 2024

Fingas, Joe, "Personal data for 533 million Facebook users leaks on the web", https://www.engadget.com/facebook-533-million-user-persona l-data-leak-180156777.html/, April 3, 2021, Accessed 11, June 2024.

7   Fanning, Tom & Easterly, Jen, "The Attack on Colonial Pipeline: What We've Learned & What We've Done Over the Past Two Years," https:// www.cisa.gov/news-events/news/attack-colonial-pipeline-what-wev e-learned-what-weve-done-over-past-two-years, May 7, 2023, Accessed 11. June 2024.

CYBERSECURITY, "What the cyber-attack on the US oil and gas pipeline means and how to increase security,", https://www.weforum. org/agenda/2021/05/cyber-attack-on-the-us-major-oil-and-gas-pipeline -what-it-means-for-cybersecurity/, May 10, 2021, Accessed 11. June 2024.

Congressional Research Service, "Colonial Pipeline: The Darkside Strikes", https://crsreports.congress.gov/product/pdf/IN/IN11667#:~:text=URL

%3A%20https%3A%2F%2Fcrsreports.congress.gov%2Fproduct%2F-pdf%2FIN%2FIN11667%0AVisible%3A%200%25%20, May 11, 2021, Accessed 11. June 2024.

Wikipedia, "Colonial Pipeline ransomware attack", https://en.wikipe-dia.org/wiki/Colonial_Pipeline_ransomware_attack, Accessed 11. June 2024.

8   Arghire, Ionut, "Celebrities Found in Unprotected Real Estate Database Exposing 1.5 Billion Records", https://www.securityweek.com/celebrities-found-in-unprotected-real-estate-database-exposing-1-5-billion-records/, December 21, 2023, Accessed 11 June 2024.

Bizga, Alina, "Massive real estate database exposes 1.5 billion records on-line; Ownership data of celebrities and public figures gets leaked", https://www.bitdefender.com/blog/hotforsecurity/massive-real-estate-databas-e-exposes-1-5-billion-records-online-ownership-data-of-celebrities-and-public-figures-gets-leaked/, December 20, 2023, Accessed 11 June 2024.

Fowler, Jeremiah, "1.5 Billion Records Leaked in Real Estate Wealth Network Data Breach", https://www.vpnmentor.com/news/report-realestatewealth network-breach/, December 19, 2023, Accessed 11 June 2024.

SCMagazine, "Over 1.5B Real Estate Wealth Network records exposed by insecure Database", https://www.scmagazine.com/brief/over-1-5 b-real-estate-wealth-network-records-_exposed-by-insecure-database, December 22, 2023, Accessed 11 June 2024.

Hackread, "Data Leak Exposes 1.5 Billion Real Estate Records, Including Elon Musk, Kylie Jenner», https://hackread.com/data-leak-exposes-rea l-estate-records-elon-musk-trump/, December 20, 2023, Accessed 11 June 2024.

9   Press Release, "UnitedHealth Group Updates on Change Healthcare Cyberattack", https://www.unitedhealthgroup.com/newsroom/2024/2 024-04-22-uhg-updates-on-change-healthcare-cyberattack.html, April 22, 2024, Access 11, June 2024.

U.S. Department of Health and Human Services, "HHS Statement Regarding the Cyberattack on Change Healthcare", https://www.hhs.

gov/about/news/2024/03/05/hhs-statement-regarding-the-cyberattac k-on-change-healthcare.html, Accessed 11, June 2024.

Faircloth, Fran & Gersh, Deborah & McNicholas, Edward & Moundas, Christina & Romig, Jennifer, "Change Healthcare Cyberattack: HHS OCR Publishes Early Guidance on Breach and UnitedHealth Group Provides Critical Status Update", https://www.ropesgray.com/en/in-sights/alerts/2024/04/change-healthcare-cyberattack-hhs-ocr-publis hes-early-guidance-on-breach-and-unitedhealth-group, April 30, 2024, Accessed 11, June 2024.

10   National Institute of Standards and Technology (NIST). (2024). "The NIST Cybersecurity Framework (CSF) 2.0.", https://nvlpubs.nist.gov/ nistpubs/CSWP/NIST.CSWP.29.pdf, February 26, 2024, Access on June 12, 2024

11   National Institute of Standards and Technology (NIST). "Cybersecurity Framework." NIST, n.d., [https://www.nist.gov/cyberframework] (https://www.nist.gov/cyberframework). 07/06/2024.

12   International Organization for Standardization (ISO). "ISO/IEC 27001 Information Security Management." ISO, n.d., [https://www.iso.org/ isoiec-27001-information-security.html](https://www.iso.org/isoiec-2700 1-information-security.html). 07/06/2024.

13   Center for Internet Security (CIS). "CIS Critical Security Controls." CIS, n.d., [https://www.cisecurity.org/controls](https://www.cisecurity. org/controls). 07/06/2024.

14   ISACA. "COBIT Framework for Governance and Management of Enterprise IT." ISACA, n.d., [https://www.isaca.org/resources/cobit] (https://www.isaca.org/resources/cobit). 07/06/2024

15   AXELOS. "ITIL Best Practice Solutions." AXELOS, n.d., [https:// www.axelos.com/best-practice-solutions/itil](https://www.axelos.com/ best-practice-solutions/itil). 07/06/2024

16   CMMI Institute. "CMMI Cyber Maturity Platform." CMMI Institute, n.d., [https://cmmiinstitute.com/cmmi/cybermaturityplatform](https:// cmmiinstitute.com/cmmi/cybermaturityplatform). 07/06/2024.

17 PCI Security Standards Council. "PCI Security Standards Council." PCI Security Standards Council, n.d., https://www.pcisecuritystandards.org/pci_security/. 07/06/2024.

18 FAIR Institute. "FAIR Risk Management." FAIR Institute, n.d., https://www.fairinstitute.org/fair-risk-management. 07/06/2024.

19 Office of the Under Secretary of Defense for Acquisition and Sustainment. "Cybersecurity Maturity Model Certification (CMMC)." Office of the Under Secretary of Defense for Acquisition and Sustainment, n.d., https://www.acq.osd.mil/cmmc/. 07/06/2024.

20 Information Security Forum (ISF). "Standard of Good Practice for Information Security." ISF, n.d., https://www.securityforum.org/solutions/standard-of-good-practice/. 07/06/2024.

21 SANS Institute. "Critical Security Controls." SANS Institute, n.d., https://www.sans.org/critical-security-controls/. 07/06/2024.

22 U.S. Department of Homeland Security. "Federal Information Security Management Act (FISMA)." U.S. Department of Homeland Security, n.d., https://www.dhs.gov/fisma. 07/06/2024.

23 CompTIA. "Security+ (SY0-601) Certification." CompTIA, n.d., https://www.comptia.org/certifications/security. 07/06/2024.

24 CompTIA. "Cybersecurity Analyst (CySA+) Certification." CompTIA, n.d., https://www.comptia.org/certifications/cybersecurity-analyst. 07/06/2024

25 (ISC)². "CISSP - Certified Information Systems Security Professional." (ISC)², n.d., https://www.isc2.org/Certifications/CISSP. 07/06/2024.

26 (ISC)² and Cloud Security Alliance (CSA). "Certified Cloud Security Professional (CCSP)." (ISC)², n.d., https://www.isc2.org/Certifications/CCSP. 07/06/2024.

27 ISACA. "Certified Information Security Manager (CISM)." ISACA, n.d., https://www.isaca.org/credentialing/cism. 07/06/2024.

28 ISACA. "Certified Information Systems Auditor (CISA)." ISACA, n.d., https://www.isaca.org/credentialing/cisa. 07/06/2024.

29 EC-Council. "Certified Incident Handler (ECIH)." EC-Council, n.d., https://www.eccouncil.org/programs/certified-incident-handler-ecih/. 07/06/2024.

30 EC-Council. "Certified Ethical Hacker (CEH)." EC-Council, n.d., https://www.eccouncil.org/programs/certified-ethical-hacker-ceh/. 07/06/2024.

31 Offensive Security. "Offensive Security Certified Professional (OSCP)." Offensive Security, n.d., https://www.offensive-security.com/pwk-oscp/. 07/06/2024.

32 Global Information Assurance Certification (GIAC). "GIAC Security Essentials (GSEC)." GIAC, n.d., https://www.giac.org/certifications/security-essentials-gsec/. 07/06/2024.

33 Cisco. "Cisco Certified CyberOps Associate." Cisco, n.d., https://www.cisco.com/c/en/us/training-events/training-certifications/certifications/associate/cyberops-associate.html. 07/06/2024.

34 ISACA. "Certified in Risk and Information Systems Control (CRISC)." ISACA, n.d., https://www.isaca.org/credentialing/crisc. 07/06/2024.

35 Amazon Web Services (AWS). "AWS Certified Security – Specialty." Amazon Web Services, n.d., https://aws.amazon.com/certification/certified-security-specialty/. 07/06/2024.